Risen

*Modern Day Eye Witness Accounts of
People Who Have Seen Jesus Face to Face*

David Holdaway

ISBN: 978-1-914173-04-2

E–mail: davidholdaway1@aol.com
www.davidholdway.org.uk

www.lifepublications.org.uk

Contents

*Just two words have changed everything forever
in our world.
They are two three word phrases in English but in the
language of the New Testament they are
just one word each:*

"Tetelestai"

which means

"It is finished."

*It is what Jesus cried out on the cross moments before
He died and means the debt and price of sin has been paid.
It means that the greatest need of every person, which is
forgiveness, can now be received from God.*

The other word is

"Egerthe"

which means

"He is risen."

*Jesus is alive and rose from the dead and this
changes everything.*

*Jesus died to give His life for us and has risen
to give His life to us.*

1

Jesus is Alive

"Don't confuse me with the evidence, my mind is made up."

A man who thought he was dead went to see a psychiatrist. The doctor spent many hours and sessions trying to convince him he was not dead but very much alive, nothing however, seemed to work. Finally, he tried one last approach. He took out his medical books and proceeded to show the patient that dead men don't bleed. After several more hours of tedious explanation he seemed to have convinced the patient.

"Do you now agree with me that dead men don't bleed?" the doctor asked. "Yes, I do," the patient replied.

"Very well, then," the doctor said. He took out a pin and pricked the patient's finger. Out came a trickle of blood. The doctor smiled and asked, "What does that tell you?"

"Oh my goodness!" the patient exclaimed as he stared incredulously at his finger. "Dead men do bleed."

It was the American and political leader William James Bryan who insightfully observed, "A great number of people think they are thinking, when they are merely rearranging their prejudices."

Wherever you travel in the world you will meet countless people who will tell you that Jesus is alive and He has changed their lives. No matter what country, colour, language or culture, the work of the Holy Spirit in convicting of sin and making known a risen Jesus is the same.

Everywhere in our world sin and its effects are the same – but so is the work of the Holy Spirit. The name of the risen Jesus transforms people in any land and heals and delivers in any language and culture.

One of the great joys of travelling to other nations is meeting others who know the same Jesus as I do but their background and culture is completely different; yet we know we belong to the same spiritual family.

This is not only true geographically but also historically. We sing hymns and recite creeds that were written hundreds and even thousands of years ago and we do it with the same joy and passion as those who have done so down the centuries because we share the same faith and experience of God.

Every day in our world more than 100,000 people are being saved and becoming followers of the Risen Jesus. Right now as you read this someone is being healed and set free and knowing the amazing peace and joy of being forgiven by Jesus because He is alive.

2

Jesus is Alive and That Changes Everything

Confucius is dead
Buddha is dead
Krishna is dead
Mohammed is dead
Gandhi is dead
Caesar is dead
Alexander the Great is dead
Napoleon is dead
Hitler is dead
Stalin is dead
Lenin is dead
Marx is dead
Mao is dead

Jesus is Alive!

- *Which religion is right or are they all wrong?*
- *Did God make man or did man make God?*
- *Is there life after death and what will happen when I die?*
- *What is the truth or is truth whatever we want it to be?*

When I was a young lad my parents believed in God but they did not become Christians until many years later. My grandparents had some Roman Catholic influence but not enough for them to go to church, and I had aunties who were seriously into Spiritism and the Jehovah's Witnesses. In our town we have one of the oldest Mormon churches in the country and some famous Mormons today have their ancestors buried in one of the town's cemeteries. My brother and I came under the church's influence because we attended Scouts there. We also went to the local Baptist church and Sunday School, and my best friend in school was a Muslim.

There were also atheists and agnostics in the family with my dad's best friend a hurt and angry unbeliever because of personal tragedy in his life.

I guess I have always asked lots of questions and I remember as a child lying in bed wondering what happened to people when they died?

As I grew older I wondered if God really did exist and if He did which religion represented Him or maybe they all did? Yet they couldn't all be right because they said contradictory things about Him.

It really boiled down to this, who was telling the truth and even more importantly what is Truth? I was to discover some years later that ultimate truth is not found in a religion or a philosophy or a science but in a person. This is why to know God is far more than just reason and logic, it involves relationship.

When Jesus said to Pontius Pilate, *"I tell you the truth."* Pilate's immediate response was, *"What is truth?"* It's the reply of a seasoned and hardened politician, someone who has climbed the greasy pole of power. He didn't ask the question to get an answer because he had probably given up believing there was one. What is so sad is that the *Truth* was standing just six feet in front of him and he couldn't see it or be bothered to investigate it.

Jesus said that He was *"the truth, the way and the life"* and the only way to truly know God. Other religions and belief systems may be able to tell you some things about God but only Jesus fully reveals Him.

These are amazing claims that Jesus made but besides His profound teaching and amazing miracles is there anything else He did to back them up? The answer is yes, He died and rose again from the dead. His physical bodily resurrection is the supreme evidence of everything He taught and claimed.

Some time ago I was visiting my daughter who lived near a busy cemetery in the centre of Cardiff, Wales. The graveyard was huge and people would walk through it using it as a short cut. I decided to have a walk around and took note that the gates would be locked in about an hours' time. After about thirty minutes I realised I was lost and unsure how to get out. The gate and fence were too high to climb over and I began to panic a little. Then humorously it dawned on me that I was lost in a place surrounded by hundreds of people who probably knew the way out, but there was a big problem, none of them could help me because they were all dead.

I eventually found the exit in time but couldn't help reflecting on how there were so many people around me, buried there, but of course, they were no help to me.

Now, just imagine for a moment you were hopelessly lost and your eternal destiny was dependant on finding the right way. As you are searching you come across all the greatest religious leaders, scientists, philosophers and thinkers there have ever been and they all claim to know the way but there's a problem, they are all dead except one, who did die but rose again. So which one would you ask and follow?

3

The Evidence is Overwhelming

Scientific proof requires observation and being able to repeat what took place. No one alive today was there when Jesus rose from the dead and no one has risen like Him since because He rose never to die again and in the power of an indestructible life.

Therefore science can neither prove nor disprove Jesus' resurrection, so we have to judge whether it happened or not on the evidence.

In a court of law the Judge and jury were not at the scene of the crime or saw the event under examination but have to make a decision based upon the evidence before them. There are two different types of evidence, eye witness and circumstantial, which includes forensics. In Jesus' resurrection we have an incredible amount of both.

Eye Witness Testimony

Jesus made at least ten resurrection appearances. On one occasion Jesus appeared to more than 500 people at one time.

He also appeared to those who were hostile or unconvinced. Saul of Tarsus was a persecutor of the church and despised Christ and His followers. It was a life-shattering as well as life changing experience when Jesus appeared to him. Although at the time he was not a disciple, he later became the Apostle Paul, one of the greatest witnesses for the resurrection of Jesus and leaders of the church he had once tried to destroy.

Another fascinating detail is what happened to Jesus' half-brothers Jude and James. We read in the gospels that they were antagonistic towards Him during His ministry and did not believe His claims. However, they later became leaders within the church and wrote two of the books in the New Testament. What could have accounted for this amazing change? They saw Jesus alive again after His crucifixion.

There are well over three hundred verses in the New Testament which are concerned with the subject of Jesus' resurrection. Paul was the first to write about it within just a few years of Jesus rising from the dead, 1 Corinthians 15.

When several people have seen something and later write it down one of the signs of truth is that they are in agreement but are not replicas of each other. If the accounts were all identical in every aspect we would suspect collusion. There are variations because each witness sees what took place from their own perspective and understanding and gives different insights and aspects.

You wouldn't believe the number of other crazy theories used to try and prove that Jesus did not rise from the dead. Some have said the disciples stole the body – even after the tomb was sealed and guarded. How could they have when the tomb was sealed and protected by Roman soldiers? And why would they give their lives for a corpse? And how did so many people see Him alive afterwards?

Others have said the women simply went to the wrong tomb. But this was a private tomb, easily identified and some of them had already been there when the body was laid inside a few days before. If Jesus' body was still in a tomb all the authorities had to do was produce it, but they couldn't because He was now alive.

When evidence is given, eye witness accounts are invaluable, but that, as I have said, is not the only kind of evidence.

Circumstantial evidence

a). Jews who became believers changed their day of worship from a Saturday to a Sunday because Jesus rose from the dead on Sunday, the first day of the week.

When you see how passionately Jews still revere and guard the Sabbath you realise how big this is.

b). Jesus' disciples were transformed from fearful frightened men to being willing to lay down their lives for their belief that Jesus died and rose again.

Most of them suffered horrible deaths and they died not surrounded by their friends to encourage them, but on their own attacked by those who hated them for what they taught and preached.

c). The amazing growth of the church – today there are over two billion people who acknowledge Jesus as Lord and Saviour.

d). Signs and wonders were done and are still being done in Jesus' name because He is alive.

Some people have a big problem with Jesus' resurrection because they can't explain it from a purely natural understanding. They were not there to see it happen and they cannot recreate it. What's incredibly significant is that so many in the legal profession and some of the most brilliant legal minds that have ever lived believe Jesus physically rose from the dead after examining the evidence. They are much better placed than even scientists to analyse the information because their minds are trained to forensically look at all the evidence and possibilities. They understand evidence and proof and spend their lives studying it.

Here are some famous lawyers

• Professor Simon Greenleaf was the Royal Professor of Law at Harvard University and one of the greatest legal minds that ever lived. He wrote a famous book entitled, *A Treatise on the Law of Evidence*, considered by many the greatest legal volume ever written. Greenleaf believed the resurrection of Jesus Christ was a hoax and he determined, once and for all, to expose it as a "myth". After thoroughly examining the evidence he came to the exact opposite conclusion! He wrote a book entitled, *An Examination of the Testimony of the Four Evangelists by the Rules of Evidence Administered in the Courts of Justice*, in which he emphatically stated:

> *It was impossible that the apostles could have persisted in affirming the truths they had narrated, had not **Jesus Christ actually risen from the dead.***

Greenleaf concluded that according to the jurisdiction of legal evidence the resurrection of Jesus Christ was the best supported event in all of history! And not only that, Dr Greenleaf was so convinced by the overwhelming evidence that he committed his life to Jesus Christ!

• Lord Darling, former Chief Justice of England, stated after investigating the evidence of the resurrection, *"there exists such **overwhelming evidence**, positive and negative, factual and circumstantial, that no intelligent jury in the world could fail to bring in a verdict that the resurrection story is true."*

• *The Guinness Book of Records* record-holder for the most successful trial lawyer, Sir Lionel Luckhoo, after examining the evidence for Christ's resurrection he concluded it was true and became a Christian and follower of Jesus.

• Sir Edward Clarke, a former attorney for King's Court stated regarding the legal and historical evidence for the resurrection;

> *As a lawyer I have made a prolonged study of the evidences for the events of the first Easter Day. To me the evidence is conclusive, and over and over again in the High Court I have secured the verdict on evidence not nearly so compelling. Inference follows on evidence, and a truthful witness is always artless and distains effect. The Gospel evidence for the resurrection is of this class, and as a lawyer I accept it unreservedly as the testimony of truthful men to facts they were able to substantiate.*

And scientists who believe in God

In the hundred years between 1900 and 2000 AD 89.5 per cent of those awarded a Nobel Prize believed in God. Only 10.5 per cent identified as atheist or agnostic.

If you were to exclude the Nobel Prize for literature from the statistics then the numbers for awards for Peace, Chemistry, Physics, Medicine and Economics is closer to 95 per cent who believe in God and most fervently believe in the resurrection of Jesus Christ.

Jesus is Alive – Modern Day Encounters

Risen

4

Nasir Saddiki

"God if you are real don't let me die"

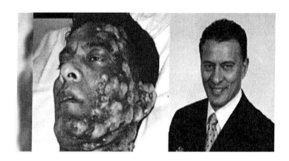

Dr Nasir Siddiki was a very wealthy 34-year-old businessman. He had almost everything life could offer as well as an incredible Muslim genealogy. His ancestor, was Abu Bakr as-Siddiq, the first caliph of the Muslim nation and a close friend of Mohammed. But all this meant little to him as he lay on his hospital bed at Toronto General Hospital, having been diagnosed with the worst case of shingles the doctors there said they had ever seen. His immune system was shutting down and they diagnosed brain damage. They gave him virtually no chance of survival.

Nasir says, *"I had started to feel unwell and blisters appeared on the side of my neck. During the night I passed out twice and my temperature was 107.6 and I was rushed to the hospital.*

"I remember two doctors coming in to see me and maybe they thought I couldn't hear them, but they said to each other 'his immune system is not fighting back. He's going to die.'

"This came a shock to me because these were the people I was putting my hope and trust in and at that point my hope was crushed. My money didn't mean anything to me, my will power and strength didn't mean anything to me, the only thing left was humility and fear. I didn't know what death held for a Muslim but I was afraid of it.

"I believed in a God but I didn't believe in Jesus as the Son of God. But even the Muslim God Allah is not a healer and Mohammed is not a healer, so I didn't cry out to Allah or Mohammed to heal me, but I cried out to God in desperation, I said, 'God, if you are real, don't let me die.' In fear I cried out."

"Later that night in the room a figure appeared at the foot of my bed, it was the outline of a person with light radiating from Him. I knew it was Jesus. He is mentioned in the Koran as a prophet and a healer. He said two things to me, 'I am the God of the Christians. I am the God of Abraham, Isaac and Jacob.'

"Something happened to me that night. The very next morning when the doctors returned they noticed the blisters on my face had stopped growing. They said they didn't understand the remission. I told them that I didn't know how to tell them, but Jesus came to my bed last night.

"They didn't believe me but couldn't understand my amazing recovery and my case was to be a test case in Toronto medical circles as to how I was still alive.

"I had improved so much they said I could go home and I left the hospital with a case full of medicine and a diagnosis of further pain and blisters.

"Even though I was greatly improved my face and neck still looked hideous and disfigured and 75-years-old. I awoke one morning a few days later at 6am and turned on the television to hear two men discussing if Jesus was the Son of God. They said He certainly was and explained how He lived and taught and healed the sick and died on a cross for our sins and rose again from the dead.

"As a Muslim I believed that the only way of forgiveness and heaven was by my good works exceeding my bad ones, or by Jihad and giving my life for my God. Now I was hearing that God loved me so much that He gave His life for me in His Son Jesus Christ.

"I got on my knees and asked God to forgive me and I gave my life to Jesus Christ."

The next morning all the blisters fell from Nasir's face and neck and he was completely healed and restored. From this time on Nasir's passion has been to serve Jesus. He and his wife founded *Wisdom Ministries* in Tulsa, Oklahoma, and teach and share their story all around the world.

Risen

5

Chris Lambrianou
Escape From The Kray Madness

As a young East End tear away, Chris Lambrianou was caught up in the dark world of violent crime, armed robbery, safe blowing, protection rackets, fraud and attempted murder. He became a henchman for the evil Kray twins who terrorized the East End of London during the 1960s.

In the foreword to his book *Escape from the Kray Madness,* Lambrianou's probation officer describes him as a bear of a man, of powerful physique and compelling personality. He says, "It is easy to see the figure he cut in the criminal culture of the sixties which were the years of the London gang wars and ascendency of the notorious Kray twins. By then he had already served several prison sentences, borstal, detention centre and three years at an approved school from the age of eleven."

Lambrianou was convicted at the Old Bailey in 1969 along with the Krays and other members of "The Firm". He was sentenced to life imprisonment for his part in the murder of Jack the Hat McVitie and was told he would serve a minimum of 15 years.

The following years were a nightmarish existence in maximum security prisons. At times he became like a wild man and was moved from one jail to another in an effort to control him.

By 1975 he had served six years of his sentence and had done a lot of soul searching and read a lot of what he says was enlightening and religious literature. One Sunday evening, he was lying on his prison bed listening to the radio and heard the distinctive voice of Bob Dylan singing on a record on a landing below. Chris says, "I tried listening to what was on the radio but the words of the record kept invading my mind, making it hard to concentrate,

> *Knock knock knocking on heaven's door...*
> *Ma, take these guns off me...*
> *I can't use them any more...*
> *It's getting dark... Too dark to see...*
> *And I feel I am knocking on heaven's door..."*

He switched off the radio and lay on his bed, eyes closed, thinking how much the words meant to him. *"Take these guns... I can't use them anymore..."*

Over and over the record played as he lay there thinking of all the wasted years of his life. He says,

"Suddenly, I felt my heart pounding and then it was as if a thick, black cloud descended on my cell enveloping me, an evil clammy darkness so real, so physical, I could almost touch it. I felt blood surging through my veins, a boiling molten scarlet blood and I turned and twisted on my bed fighting the anger, the frightening evil fury, raging inside me. And then the voices started again in my head, 'You are never getting out...You gave your life away to the Krays. You are never getting out. This is forever...Think how you feel now. This emptiness, this nothingness, this loneliness. This is how you are going to feel forever. It's never going to change.'"

Frightened by the voices and the force inside him he jumped off the bed and went to the mirror. He says, "Looking back at me was a scowling, snarling, sneering beast, shocking in its ugliness and it was screaming, 'Kill yourself, you're never getting out. End it all.'"

Somewhere else, in what he called his twisted soul, he heard another voice, faint but insistent, pleading with him to drag himself out of the madness, to do something positive to break the evil spell before it pulled him over the line and past the point of no return.

He then remembered some books given to him by another prisoner and went to a box under his bed where his eyes fell on a Gideon Bible which he didn't know was there. He says,

"I threw it down and looked for something else. I went through a dozen books and then for some reason I could not understand, I found myself picking up the Bible again. I started reading in Genesis but gave up after a couple of minutes, however I couldn't let the book go. I didn't know what it was but there was something there, a power. I put the Bible under my pillow, thinking that if there were any good thoughts in the book, they would come through to me.

"I lay in the darkness, exhausted but unable to sleep. I kept thinking of the Bible, saying over and over to myself, 'If there is anybody there, let me know. I don't believe, but if there is someone there, please let me know.' I didn't feel comfortable with the Bible under the pillow. I wanted it nearer. I took it and clutched it against my heart and closed my eyes, fighting to control the rage burning inside me. Finally, mercifully, I dropped off to sleep. It was around three in the morning, I had been fighting the devil for nine hours."

When he awoke he took the Bible with him stuffed down his trousers. He had an overwhelming desire to have it close to him all day. He started reading it secretly in his cell and thinking about Jesus more and more.

At the end of each day he would get down on his hands and knees and pray thanking the Lord for the day. He says, "I was not a religious fanatic and I was not off my trolley. I felt I was the sanest I'd been in my whole life."

A few months later he was moved to a new prison. He was still reading the Bible but the 'raging beast' was still in him if things did not go his way.

One night, as he lay on his bed, he began to cry thick tears of remorse for the world he had lost and destroyed and for all the loved ones he had left in pain. He describes what happened next,

"And then, through my tears, I saw three people in the corner of the cell. They looked Middle Eastern and wearing dark raincoats. The one in the middle, the only one I clearly remember, had long, jet black hair and a trimmed beard; under his raincoat, he was wearing a European suit with a white shirt and tie. And he had the most wonderful, warm welcoming eyes I'd ever seen. He had such a clarity of vision I knew he was a man of purpose.

"Through my tears I said to him, 'How do I put it right? I have run through my life, wrecking everything. I've made a terrible, terrible mess. I'm so sorry.' The bearded man (who he said later he knew was Jesus) said simply, 'follow us' then he and the other two men vanished as quickly as they had come."

He started attending church in the prison as his life began to turn around. His life and attitude so changed over time that he was granted parole. His faith and witness became stronger and he managed to get work at the Ley Community in Oxfordshire, a rehabilitation centre for alcohol and drug abusers.

At the end of his fascinating book he says,

> "I'm proud of what I am achieving at the Ley. I'm proud that I had the courage to write this book. And I'm proud to be a Christian. With God's guidance, I shall continue to be one. The prodigal son said, *'Shall I leave the swine and return to my father's house, perhaps he will give me a job on the land. When he was far off his father saw him and ran to greet him,'"* (Luke 15:11-32).

Chris's story is a fascinating account of no matter who we are and what we have done, God's love reaches out to us. It is fitting he ends with the story of the prodigal son because it reminds us that when we take one step towards God, He comes running towards us.

6

Professor Richard Flashman
"I realised that if there was no God there was no hope."

Richard Flashman is an associate professor of practical theology and teaches in Brooklyn, N.Y., at the Charles L. Feinberg Centre for Messianic Jewish Studies, an extension of Talbot School of Theology in partnership with *Chosen People Ministries.*

He says, "I remember a conversation with my mother and she was encouraging me to go to bed early and get a good night's sleep. So I said, 'Mum, why should I go to bed early and get a good night's sleep?' She said, 'So that you can get up and be refreshed and do well in school.' I said, 'Why do I need to do well in school?' She said, 'So that you can go to a good college.' And I said, 'Why do I need to go to a good college?' She said, 'So you can get a good job.' I replied, 'But why do I need a good job?' She said, 'So that you can have a family and a house and the nice things of life.' So I said, 'If I have all those things then what?' She said, 'Then – nothing, that's it.' I said, 'Is that all there is?'

"Being the only son of a Jewish mother I was made to feel that I was the centre of Universe, it was all about me and I wanted it to be all about me.

"I sought the approval and affirmation and the confirmation of these things from other people, that in fact it was about me and that I was the centre of the universe.

"I went to a private school and we had to study the life of Jesus and I didn't even like Jesus. So I wanted to hear from my Rabbi why we don't believe in Jesus. He explained that when the Messiah comes we will have peace and that Jesus couldn't be the Messiah because since Jesus has already come and there is no peace He could not be the Messiah. That satisfied me for the next seven years. I was totally satisfied with that answer and it made sense to me.

"In college I became a theoretical Marxist. I believed that what the world needed was judicial social change, instead of people competing against each other in the market place, that Government would come and create an equal playing field, even more than that, create equal outcomes for everyone in the culture. We could get rid of the competitiveness and the adversarial relationships that I saw in life, and we could work towards co-operation and we could create a better world together.

"I really wanted to make a better world. I saw this as a source of significance and the purpose of my life – that I could help bring about a better world for mankind.

"The only problem with my convictions about social change and making a better world was the problem of the brokenness in people. In my own personal brokenness I saw my own selfish pride, my own lust, my own greed and I saw those things in other people. I saw it in the world around me and if there was something wrong within us, if there was something wrong with people then changing social systems wouldn't make any real difference. It would be just the same thing over and over again.

"So in my first year of college I heard a knock on the door, I opened the door and there was a young man, he looked at me and said, 'Hi, my name is Paul, and I'd like to talk to you about establishing a personal relationship with Jesus Christ.' I was taken by surprise and said, 'I'm sorry I am Jewish,' and he said, 'that's ok, so was Jesus.' I said, 'Yeah, yeah you are right, come on in.' I invited him in to the room and also invited some of my Jewish friends from down the hall to come and join us and he began to explain to us that Jesus was the Jewish Messiah.

"But the questions I came to college with stayed with me and I realised that if there was no God there was no hope. That led me on a search and in the process of that search I came across the prophecy in the 53rd chapter of Isaiah and I remember thinking to myself *'What's Jesus doing in my Bible?'* I was surprised as I read it that this was from the Prophet Isaiah, the Jewish prophet. And I began to think, *'Why didn't the Rabbi tell me about this? Why didn't he tell me that there was a picture of the Messiah other than the Messiah bringing peace, but a Messiah who was going to suffer and die for us?'*

"After college, in order to make extra money, I would work nights and weekends for a kosher caterer in Boston. One night, April 30, 1980, I was serving at a charity dinner at Temple Sinai in Marblehead, Massachusetts. I was asked if I would pack up the truck so everybody else could go home and just I would be left, and I said, that's fine. So everybody left as the ladies continued their fund raiser in the building and I was outside with a cup of coffee and a cigarette just thinking about life.

"All of a sudden, inside the synagogue the women started praying. Their prayers began to remind me of my own searching, my own struggle, my own journey that I was on and I started thinking about Jewish history, about King David and about Jesus, is He really the Messiah? Is it really important who the Messiah is? Is Jesus the Son of God? Is He God? Did He ever say that He is God? Couldn't He just have meant that He was close to God and intimate with God? And I thought what difference does that make with the Name of God as long as we live a good life?

"And as I was thinking these things I was walking around the Temple parking lot and I got to the end of the parking lot, and when I got there and looked up, before me is a gathering of light and the light forms a figure of a man and the man is all in the light and He is in front of a cross, not on the cross but in front of a cross, and it's all brightly illuminated in front of me about 20 yards away from me as big as life. And I looked up and I saw the figure, and I said, 'Oh my God, it is Jesus Christ'.

"My hands were shaking and I'm shaking my head as I make my way home. Did I really see this? And it scared me so much I decided to try and put it out of my mind. So I spent the next couple of weeks just partying and going out to bars and trying to forget about what had happened. I did this for the next couple of weeks, just getting drunk and trying to forget.

"I woke up one morning, I was living at home at the time and I was getting some orange juice in the kitchen and my mother looked at me and said, 'Rich, what are you running away from?'

"So I came to realise that I wasn't the centre of the universe, that God was; that it wasn't about me but that it was about Him. It was about me investing my life in His purposes that He had for me. And that gave me such a feeling of meaning and purpose in my life it was beyond anything I could ever have dreamt of. I never thought I'd get the answers but now I realised that there's a God and that He loves me and that love sets me free to love and serve others and to love and serve Him."

Risen

7

Hermann Bonnke

"Hermann, I am so glad you are coming."

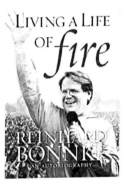 

In his autobiography *Living a Life of Fire*, the great German Evangelist Reinhard Bonnke told about the dramatic encounter his father, Hermann Bonnke, had with Jesus Christ when he saw Him face to face.

His father had been an officer in the Germany army during the World War II and was captured towards the end of the war and put in a British prisoner of war camp.

Reinhard says,

"Not feeling well, my father Hermann Bonnke lay in his prison bunk staring at the wood slats of the bed a few inches above his nose. He had been excused from work detail, which allowed him to spend some precious time alone in the British prison barracks.

"He thought of how many millions of prisoners had lain awake in claustrophobic quarters like this throughout the hellish war years. Victims of the Nazi regime. How many of them – millions of them – had died in horrible ways he wished he could erase from his mind.

"He had only recently learned of Hitler's Final Solution and was still in shock over it. The extermination of Jews appalled him beyond words. As a Pentecostal believer, he had regarded the Jews as the chosen people through whom God had revealed the Messiah, the saviour of all mankind. Knowing he had served a government that had tried to exterminate all of them left him permanently shaken. It haunted his thoughts and even his dreams at night.

"How the descendants of the Holy Roman Empire could be transformed into the Nazi regime, he still could not fathom. But he had seen it with his own eyes, day after day, with a helpless feeling in the pit of his stomach. It had taken only ten years for Hitler to seize absolute power over his beloved Homeland. He would never live another day without regretting being German.

"He had been in this prison camp for 279 days and nights. Every minute of every day he felt the pang of longing for his wife, Meta, and his children. He saw each of their faces in his memory now, as he had seen them last in Stablack. He prayed for them by name, asking that they be preserved alive and

well, and that they be reunited by God's grace and in due time.

"He had inquired again and again through the Red Cross of their safety and whereabouts but had learned nothing. With each passing day the gnawing ache in his stomach grew stronger, whispering that they had not survived.

"Still in his confinement, he did not feel persecuted. It seemed small payment for the mega death and suffering dealt by the German army over the last few years. The trials for Nazi war crimes were even now beginning in the city of Nuremberg. He would not have to stand trial because as an officer in the Reichswehr, he had never joined the Nazi Party. But he had served in their terrible killing machine. He thought that if he were given the death penalty as a prisoner of war now, it would not be too severe. But alas, it could not atone for so many sins. The war's sweep was too massive and its evils too many for any court to ever set right.

"But there was One who kept perfect count. Not even a sparrow fell without His knowledge. The hairs of heads of every victim, not to mention of every perpetrator, had been perfectly numbered and recorded in His Divine Book. One day the Book would be opened, and everyone would stand before the Great White Throne to give account of his deeds. God alone could balance the scales of justice.

"And He had done so. In heaven there was a second Book. The Book of Life. The members of the human race would not finally stand or fall upon their own deeds – good or evil, they would be saved if their names are in this Book. This was Hermann's hope and the hope of every Christian believer on both sides of the war.

"As he lay there, in his imagination, he saw a pair of scales weighed down to the floor with an impossible debt. A tank, a bomber, a field helmet, a bayonet, an Iron Cross adorned with swastikas. Then placed on the opposite side of the scale, the old rugged cross. Under the weight of that cross the scales were balanced. This alone was the equation of Divine justice. God placed on Jesus the iniquity of us all.

"Tears ebbed from his eyes as his heart reached out to this infinite God in prayer, 'My Heavenly Father, I am yours for the remaining years of my life. No more military service for me. It is my heart's desire to preach your gospel and to serve you alone, until the day I see you face to face.'

"Across the empty barracks he heard a door quietly open and close. Someone began walking softly across the floor. The flooring softwoods creaked beneath every step. He thought perhaps it was a British guard coming to check on him, or a doctor coming to see why he had reported sick. He rolled from the bunk and stood up to face him and to his utter shock it was a man in white wearing a seamless robe and Middle Eastern sandals. He was smiling as he moved towards him, hands extended as if to embrace him.

"His hair was long and his beard full and when Hermann reached out to take his hand he saw that it was torn through with the force of a Roman nail.

"Hermann, I am so glad you are coming," the Master said, then vanished into thin air.

"Hermann fell to his knees. He could do nothing but weep for the rest of the day and night. How could the Saviour be made glad by one so guilty? Returning to his bunk, he lay down, his

soul overflowing with the peace of God that passes understanding. Until this moment it had seemed inconceivable that an imprisoned soldier of the Third Reich could receive the smile of the Lamb of God, and that the Saviour would express God's pleasure at his desire to serve Him as a minister of the Gospel. The treasure of this encounter burned like a warming fire in his heart until the day he died."

Many years later, before his death, Hermann had the joy of accompanying his son, Reinhard, on his great gospel missions across Africa.

Reinhard also posted the following blog regarding his father, which shows the compassion and love that burned in them both.

"My father, Hermann Bonnke, was young, strong and sportive. Walking by the water one day he heard a cry for help. He saw a man struggling, in danger of drowning in the water. How or why the man was there didn't matter for my father. He was a strong swimmer and without a moment's hesitation, jumped in the flood, grabbed him and saved his life.

"He brought the half drowned victim to the water's edge and began pulling him ashore, when he felt a peculiar drag. Heaving the victim to safety seemed an unexpected weight, heavy work. He could not understand why. Then he saw it. To his astonishment, he found that two more drowning people were hanging on to the first man's feet! He was saving not one but three people. Three for the price of one! And so it can be when Jesus saves one soul. Others may be in tow, often

whole families. Be encouraged. Keep praying and witnessing. The Lord will save your family and friends."

Reinhard dedicated his autobiography to his mother and father with the following words,

'For Hermann and Meta Bonnke, true parents in life, and in the Lord.'

8

Professor James Tour

A Jewish Scientist Meets Jesus

"I build molecules for a living, I can't begin to tell you how difficult that job is. I stand in awe of God because of what He has done through His creation. Only a rookie who knows nothing about science would say science takes away from faith. If you really study science, it will bring you closer to God."

James Tour is an American synthetic organic chemist, specializing in nanotechnology. He is the W.F.Chao Professor of Chemistry, Professor of Materials Science and Nano Engineering, and Professor of Computer Science at Rice University in Houston, Texas, United States.

In 2015 Tour was inducted into the National Academy of Inventors and in 2014 named among "The 50 most Influential Scientists in the World Today." In 2013 he was named "Scientist of the Year" by *R&D Magazine* and won the ACS Nano Lectureship Award from the American Chemical Society in 2012. He was ranked one of the top ten chemists in the world over the past decade by Thomson Reuters in 2009.

He was also made a fellow of the American Association for the Advancement of Science. Other notable awards won by Tour include the 2008 Feynman Prize in Nanotechnology, the NASA Space Act Award in 2008 for his development of carbon nanotube reinforced elastomers, the Arthur C. Cope Scholar Award from the American Chemical Society (ACS) for his achievements in organic chemistry in 2007 and Innovator of the Year Award in 2006.

In 2005, Tour's journal article *Directional Control in Thermally Driven Single-Molecule Nanocars* was ranked the Most Accessed Journal Article by the American Chemical Society. He has written more than 650 scholarly articles.

That's quite a resume but what Tour says about his relationship with God is even more impressive, he says, *"More than any of that what means the most to me is that I am a Jew who believes that Jesus is the Messiah."*

Here is his own story in his own words as to how he made that discovery and his encounter when he saw Jesus.

"I grew up just outside New York City and everyone I knew was Jewish and all my friends were Jewish, but when I went to University I started meeting a number of Christians who said that they were born again Christians, which to me was

sort of an odd term. I thought, 'Born again, what do you mean born again?' One person saw me in the laundry room and said 'Do you mind if I give you an illustration of the gospel?' I remember he sat there and he actually started to draw a picture of a cliff with a man on one side and another cliff with God on the other side and a great chasm between that he labelled sin.

"I looked at him and said, 'I am not a sinner, I have never killed anyone, I have never robbed a bank, how can I be a sinner?' And he had me read a verse from the Bible, '…that all have sinned and fallen short of the glory of God,' (Romans 3:23). In modern Judaism we really don't talk about sin, I don't remember ever hearing about sin in my house.

"So he turned to another passage where Jesus said, 'I say to you that everyone who looks upon a woman with lust for her has already committed adultery with her in his heart,' (Matthew 5:28).

"'Pow!' I felt as if I had been punched in the chest. Here I was in college and I would pick up these magazines and was addicted to pornography and all of a sudden something that's written in the Bible, spoken by someone who lived 2000 years ago, was calling me out on it. I felt immediately convicted and I realised that I was a sinner. How was I going to get right with God?

"We Jews know this better than anyone else, 'That without the shedding of blood there is no forgiveness of sin,' (Hebrews 9:22). The description in Isaiah 53 of how He will bear upon Himself my sin, for the things I have done. This

was the man who took this upon Himself on the Cross. The perfect God comes and gives Himself for us.

"I started to realise how Jewish the New Testament is, it's all around Jewish people. And then, on November 7, 1977, I was alone in my room and had this realisation that Yeshua (Jesus) is the one who died on the cross. And I said, 'Lord, I understand that I am a sinner, please forgive me and come into my life.'

The Encounter

"Then all of a sudden someone was in my room. I was on my knees and I opened my eyes…who was in my room? That man Jesus Christ stood in my room. There was this amazing sense of God. Jesus was in my room and I wasn't scared.

"All I started doing was weeping. The presence was so glorious because Jesus was there in my room on that day. I didn't want to get up and I had this amazing sense of forgiveness that came upon me.

"Finally I got up and I didn't know what to do, I didn't know who to tell. I was just this Jewish kid from New York City, what was I going to say?

"My cousins were shocked when I told them. 'How could you give your life to Jesus? You are Jewish?' When I told my mother how I had invited Jesus into my life she didn't say much, she was weeping, she told my father and they were not happy at all. She said, 'I don't blame them for killing Jesus after the things He said, who was He to come against those religious leaders who had dedicated their lives to helping people and to tell them they were white washed tombs? Who

is He, this young man in his thirties, to say this to scholars? He got what he deserved.'

"My mother is a very deep pensive reader. She read from Genesis to Revelation. When she got done, I asked her, 'What do you think?' She said, 'God warned us over and over again, He warned us.'

"When my daughter was about 15 my mother and father came to visit us. At one point my mother went into her room for several hours. She came out and said to me, 'Quite a young girl you have. She talked to me for quite a long time.' So my mother started reading her Bible again, both Old and New Testaments.

"One day, not long after, she called me on the phone. At the age of 72, she said, 'Jimmy, you won't believe what happened.' I said, 'What happened?' She said, 'I was just reading and it hit me, it hit me, the way He gave His life. Jesus is the Son of God."

Risen

9

Betty Baxter

A Remarkable Healing

The miraculous healing of Betty Baxter was so amazing that it was investigated by journalists and photographers, and the first paper to print the incredible story was the *Fairmount Daily Sentinel* in Minnesota, USA. Numerous affidavits and testimonials were also taken of people who were there and witnessed what took place.

Betty was born with a curve in her spine and every vertebra was out of place. The X-rays showed that the bones were twisted and matted together; therefore her nervous system was wrecked. The doctors kept her on drugs so she could endure the pain and at just nine years of age she was sent home from hospital to die.

As she lay in her darkened bedroom, her lifeless twisted body was no more than a few feet in length as she was so twisted up. Her heart had become enlarged causing her to suffer frequent heart attacks, and at times she could hardly breathe and she struggled for breath. Yet for the next few years she managed to live by the prayers and loving care of her mother and father.

When she was 14-years-old she says she heard the voice of Jesus speaking audibly to her saying, "**I am going to heal you completely on August 24th, Sunday afternoon, at three o'clock.**" So sure and excited was she that this was going to happen that she asked her mother to buy her a new dress and pair of shoes she could wear to church on the Sunday evening after Jesus healed her.

At 2pm on August 24 many friends and church members gathered in Betty's home to pray and witness her healing. They later gave sworn testimony to what they saw.

At a quarter to three Betty's mum came and sat at her bedside and Betty asked to be moved to sit in the big chair ready for what was about to happen. She was carried and her little twisted body was propped up in the chair with pillows. The room was full of people kneeling on the floor in prayer.

Betty says, *"I saw my baby brother, four years old, and I realized I was so bent that I stood only as high as he did. He knelt down by me, looked up and said, 'Sis, it's not very long now until you will be taller than me.'"*

Betty says at 3pm Jesus came,

"Suddenly, I heard a great noise as if a storm was coming up. I heard the wind as it roared. I tried to speak above the noise. 'He's coming. Don't you hear Him? He has come at last.' Then all at once the noise subsided. All was calm and quiet and I knew in this quietness Jesus would come. I sat in the big chair, a hopeless cripple. I was so hungry to see Him. All at once I saw a great, white, fleecy cloud form. It wasn't the cloud I was waiting for. Then out of the cloud stepped Jesus. It wasn't a vision, it wasn't a dream. I saw Jesus. As He came walking slowly toward me I looked on His face. The most striking thing about Jesus is His eyes. He was tall and broad and was dressed in robes glistening white. His hair was brown and parted in the middle. It fell over His shoulders in soft waves. I will never forget His eyes.

"Jesus came slowly towards me with His arms outstretched. I noticed the ugly prints of the nails in His hands. The closer He got to me the better I felt. When He came real close I began to feel very small and unworthy. I wasn't anything but a little forgotten girl who was deformed and crippled. Then all at once He smiled at me and I wasn't afraid anymore. He was my Jesus. His eyes held mine and if I ever looked into eyes filled with beauty and compassion, they were the eyes of Jesus. There aren't many people I've seen who have eyes like Jesus.

"Jesus came and stood at the side of my chair. One part of His garment was loose and it fell inside my chair and if my arms had not been paralyzed I could have touched His garment. I had thought when He came to heal me I would start talking to Him and ask Him to heal me. But I couldn't

say a word. I just looked at Him and kept my eyes on His dear face trying to tell Him how much I needed Him. He leaned down and looked up in my face and spoke softly. I can hear every word right now because it is written in my heart. He said very softly, 'Betty, you have been patient, kind and loving, I am going to promise you health, joy and happiness.' I saw Him reach out His hand and I waited. Then I felt His hand go over the knots on my spine.

"He placed His hand on the very centre of my spine on one of the large knots. All at once a hot feeling as hot as fire surged through my body. Two hot hands took my heart and squeezed it and when those hot hands let my heart go, I could breathe normal for the first time in my life. Two hot hands rubbed over the organs of my stomach and I knew my organic trouble was healed, I would not need a new kidney and I would be able to digest my food because He had healed me.

"The hot feeling ran on through my body. Then I looked at Jesus to see if He would leave me just healed inside. Jesus smiled and I felt the pressure of His hands on the knots and as His hands pressed in the middle of my spine there was a tingling sensation like I had touched a live wire. I felt this sensation like an electrical current and stood on my feet totally straight – I was healed inside and outside. In ten seconds Jesus had healed me and made me whole.

"You say, 'Betty, how did you feel when you jumped out of the chair?' You'll never know unless you once were a hopeless cripple. You'll never know unless you sat in a chair with no hope. I ran to my mother and said, 'Mom, feel, are the knots gone?' She felt up and down my spine and said,

'Yes, they are gone! I heard the bones crack and pop. Betty, you're healed! You're healed! Praise Him for it!'

"I turned around and looked back at the chair that was empty and tears rolled down my cheeks. My body felt light all over because I didn't have any pain and I had always had pain. I felt tall because I had been bent almost double with my head on my chest, the knots were gone and my spine was straight. I raised my arms and pinched one of them. My arms had feeling. They weren't paralyzed anymore. Then I looked and saw my baby brother standing in front of the chair. Big tears were rolling down his little cheeks. Looking up at me I heard him say, 'I saw Sis jump out of the big chair. I saw Jesus heal Sis.' He was really thrilled. I picked up the chair, raised it above my head and said, 'See what the God I serve can do!'

"Standing right behind my baby brother Jesus still stood. He looked at me from the soles of my feet to the top of my head. I was straight and normal. Holding my eyes with His, He began to speak slowly. He said. 'Betty, I am giving you the desire of your heart to be healed. You are normal and well. You have health now. You are completely well because I healed you.'"

Betty lived a healthy life travelling the world testifying of Jesus' love and power for the next seventy years until her death when she saw Jesus face to face once more.

Betty after she was healed.

The picture has her standing sideways to show how straight her back is and how her body was completely healed.

Invitation

If you have been moved and inspired by these stories and the evidence that Jesus is alive and desire to know Him personally, here is a prayer that will help you on that journey,

Lord Jesus Christ,

I know that I have sinned in my thoughts, words and actions.
There are many good things I have not done and many sinful things I have done.
I am sorry for my sins and now turn from everything I know to be wrong.
I put my trust in You and ask You to forgive me because You gave Your life for me upon the cross.
Gratefully I give my life back to You and ask You to come into my life.
Come as my Saviour to cleanse and forgive me.
Come as my Lord to reign over me.
Come as my Friend to be with me.
And I will serve you all the remaining years of my life.

Amen.

For more stories of people who have had amazing, life changing encounters with Jesus Christ and the full accounts of some of the stories featured here, the book *They Saw Jesus* by David Holdaway is available from: www.lifepublications.org.uk. Or by contacting lifepublications1@hotmail.co.uk

Other books by David Holdaway:
The Life of Jesus More Than a Prophet
The Life of Jesus
The Captured Heart
The Burning Heart   •
Issues of the Heart
Revival is a Heart Issue
Never Enough
Money and Spiritual Warfare
Was Jesus Rich
How to Survive and Succeed in a Financial Crisis
No More Fear
Footholds and Strongholds
How to Stand Against a Spiritual Attack
Winning over Worry
From Dying to Flying
Psalm 23: Seven Life Changing Insights
How to Know the Will of God for Your Life
What Word Does Every University Professor Spell Wrong?
Our Covenant Keeping God
Jesus the Wonder of Christmas /
The Wonder of Christmas
Laugh and Laugh Again Series Volumes 1-8

Does God Have a Sense of Humour? Does God Believe in Atheists?
Falling Asleep in Church   All Preachers Great and Small
Butt Prints in the Sand   Educated to Stupidity
The Talking Frog   How Old Would You Be...?